healing

the fabric

of the universe

an imaginal approach to arts practice

through the works of Atsushi Takenouchi
and Louise Kenward.

Carolina Diaz

This material was originally presented
as a Master's dissertation paper at
Camberwell College of Arts, University
of the Arts London in September 2011.

First published September 2012

ISBN   978-1-4717-9764-4

Eleusis Arts, London.

Contact the author at

carolina.books@gmail.com
http://www.eleusis-arts.co.uk

arts - philosophy - dance

healing

the fabric

of the universe

Abstract

This paper explores a concern with soul and the unconscious, and their place in contemporary arts practice. It examines the role of the artist in the ongoing process of actualising the archetypal dimension of the collective psyche and what James Hillman defines as *soul-making*.

The work of two currently practising artists, Atsushi Takenouchi and Louise Kenward, is discussed through the lens of Robert Romanyshyn's imaginal approach, following James Hillman, Henri Corbin and C. G. Jung. Complementary ideas are drawn from the poetics of Gaston Bachelard, the phenomenology of Maurice Merleau-Ponty and Suzi Gablik's re-enchantment of art.

The pieces are discussed in relation to the restoration of a mythic consciousness in the contemporary arts and its relevance within the context of postmodern preoccupations.

A combination of primary and secondary sources was used. Research involved direct observation of the pieces, photography, interview, and revision of bibliographic, internet and video resources, as well as catalogues.

The work is also informed by my personal experience as a butoh practitioner and student of Atsushi Takenouchi's for more than five years.

The analysis of the works and methods of these two artists reveals that a devotional attitude in arts needs not be circumscribed by adherence to organised religion or constrained by traditional forms. It also shows how, by becoming a vehicle for the archetypal dimension of the cultural psyche, an artist's practice can serve the collective while retaining its autonomy. It makes apparent that the question of *soul* is not only relevant within the context of postmodern preoccupations, but can be the answer to many of them, and highlights the role and responsibility that artists have as co-creators of culture.

Contents

After more than a century of evidence
for the existence of the unconscious
and its formative influence in all aspects of
human life, it seems naive in the extreme
not to take it into account in our ways of
knowing and researching.

R. Romanyshyn

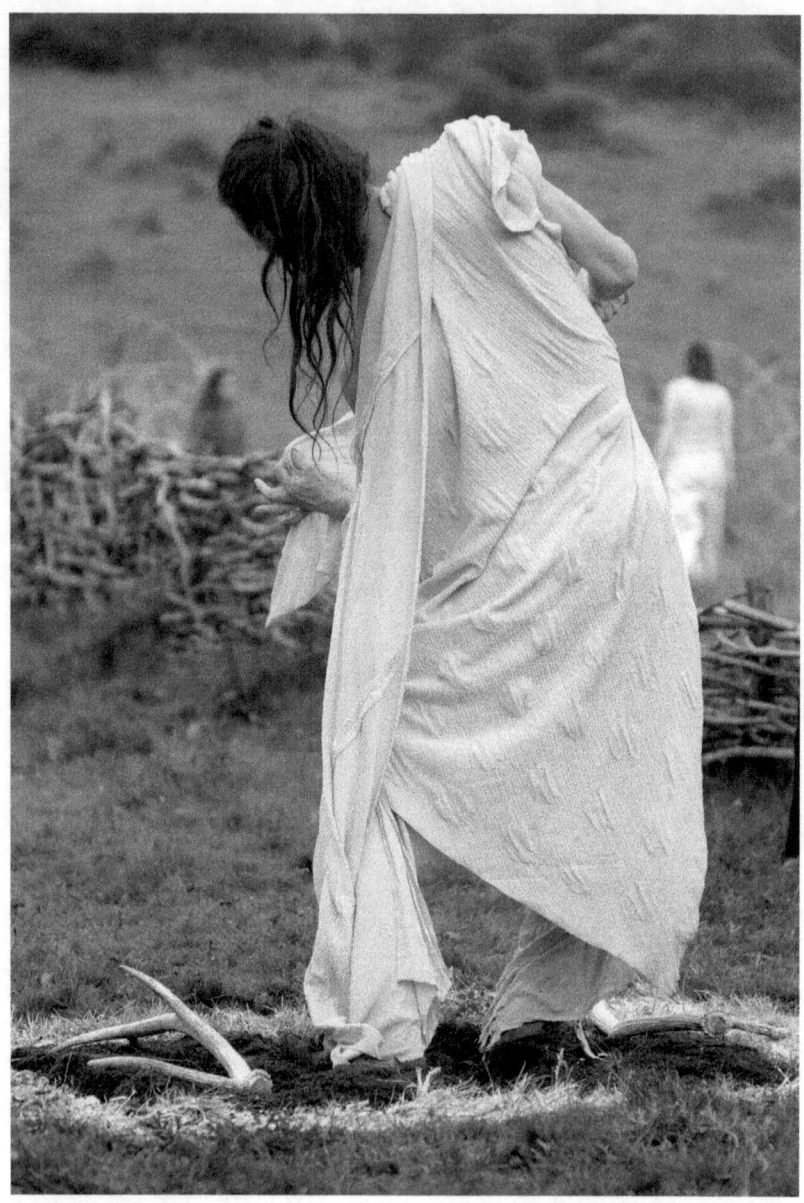

Atsushi Takenouchi in Red Earth's multimedia piece *Chalk*, performing in the South Downs near Chichester in South East England.   Photograph by Carolina Diaz.

Introduction

How can an artist, in the context of contemporary practice, make a place for the unconscious and the mythical, a place for the soul, without falling in the traps of superficial iconographic revivalism, and while maintaining autonomy from the prescribed aesthetic norms of institutionalised or traditional religious art?

About two years ago I encountered the writings of Robert Romanyshyn. In the tradition of C.G.Jung and James Hillman, he writes about the soul as a tangible dimension of psychic life. This resonated with questions that kept coming up about my own artistic practice. I was then introduced to Suzi Gablik's ideas about the necessity for a 're-enchantment' of the arts in the postmodern world, the re-conquest of a side of our experiential reality that seems to be neglected in the current arts scene, more concerned with issues of marketing and personality cult than with the ideas of service and transcendence. [1]

Although much has changed since Gablik expressed these concerns in the 1980s, particularly in the resurgence of community arts, there is still a gap that asks for attention. *Spirituality* and *soul* are still bad words that seem to raise suspicion every time they are pronounced in the context of arts or academia. Many of the attempts to introduce spiritual or mythical elements in artistic work seem uncomfortably literalistic and hollow, or as if in need to justify themselves by bringing in a touch of apologetic cynicism. With the help of Nietzsche, we managed to kill God very efficiently but our souls are still hungry.

    I wonder, is it terribly *démodé* to be concerned with the soul in the contemporary arts scene? Is there a way to put one's arts practice in the service of something other than ego, without having to adhere to sets of beliefs or aesthetic prescriptions? I acknowledge the value of community practice and its impact, but I wonder whether that is the only answer, or whether something else can be added to that. Paraphrasing Romanyshyn, I ask myself how can we go about doing one's arts practice *with soul in mind*?.

    In this stydy, I look at two pieces of work: *Cave*, by Louise Kenward, and the Butoh performance of Atsushi Takenouchi in the multimedia piece *Chalk* by Red Earth. I discuss these pieces through a simplified version of the imaginal approach that Romanyshyn outlines in his book *The wounded researcher: research with soul in mind*, adapting his imaginal methodology, re-contextualising it from its original application in the field of psychological research and into that of arts practice, and referring to the notions of soul and the imaginal in the context of depth psychology, specifically through the ideas of James Hillman and Henri Corbin.

    I acknowledge my adaptation of Romanyshyn's methodology might be an over-simplification, probably a dangerous one, and that the subject is much more complex than what I am presenting here. But an extensive extrapolation of the many ideas he presents in his book, and which happen to be all very relevant to the matter of arts practice in the postmodern world, would be well beyond the scope of this paper.

My temptation is to keep adding, my challenge is then to leave behind. I shall find comfort in Romanyshyn's admonition that research is always an unfinished work.

> *... the work of saying what asks to be spoken in one's work is never complete. We begin and we fall short and we begin again... words matter, even though they fail.*
>
> R. Romanyshyn.
> *The Wounded Researcher.*

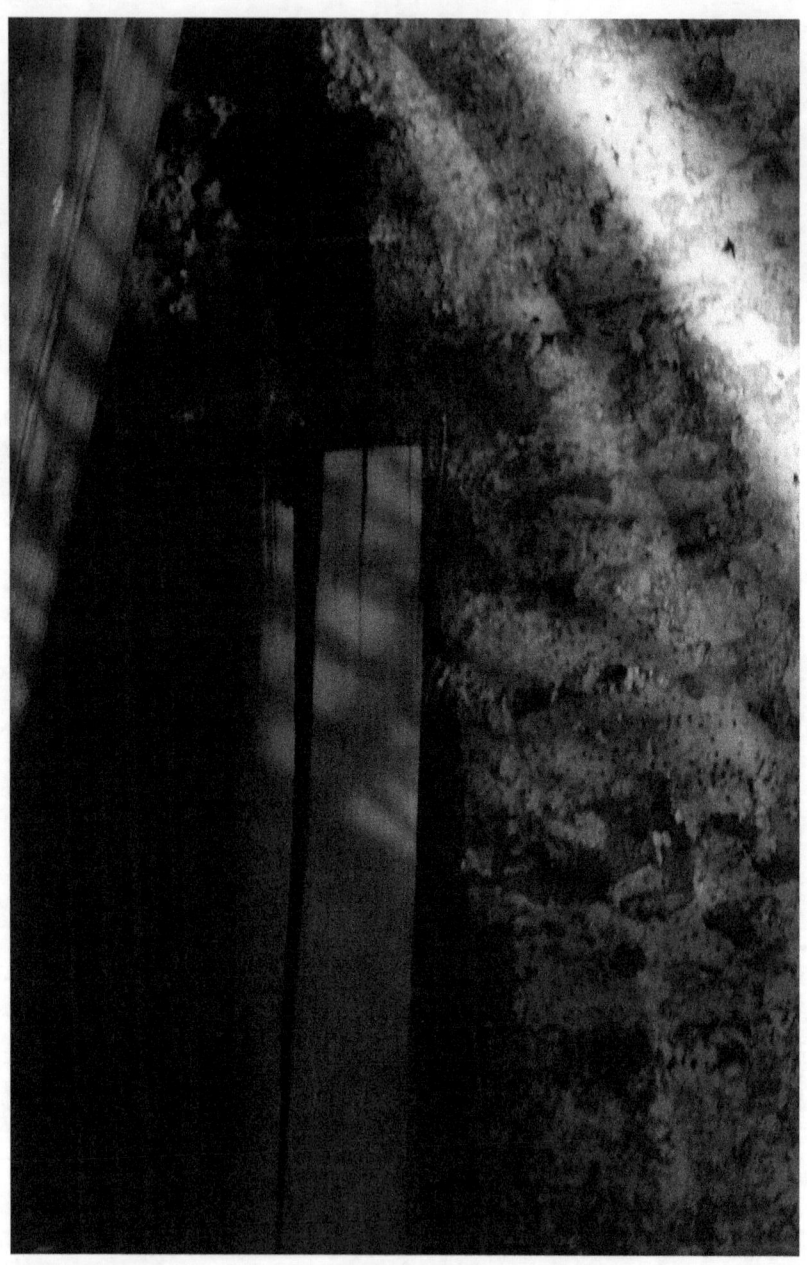

Light and shadows inside the *Cave*. Photograph by Carolina Diaz.

1. A softer kind of light: soul and the mythic consciousness

Romanyshyn defines his imaginal approach as a 'fundamental shift from the point of view of the ego to that of soul'. It is rooted in an archetypal understanding of the notion of soul or psyche, with links to Gaston Bachelard's poetics and Henri Corbin's *mundus imaginalis* .

James Hillman describes the soul as a poetic basis of the mind that experiences life as image, as myth, as meaning. A faculty that 'recognises all realities as primarily symbolic or metaphorical'. As archetypal, this substrate of consciousness is both autonomous and animistic, a term ethymologically and historically linked to *anima*, another word for soul, populated by figures or persons.

Corbin refers to this area of experience as a region or *geography* lying beyond the limits of the rational and the factual but which is not in itself imaginary, in the sense of something constructed or made up. Just as we do not fabricate our dreams but they happen to us, the figures of the psyche have their own autonomy.

The term imaginal is then favoured to acknowledge this distinction and the tendency of these figures to manifest through images, symbols and the metaphorical. For Corbin, the imaginal is related to both the world of the ancestors and that of the archetypes, the primordial images that provide the structures of our subjective experience.

Merleau-Ponty suggests that we encounter different worlds as we engage with the world in different ways. The parameters that condition our perceptions and guide our interpretations create the *realities* that we believe external and immutable. If the world comes into being as we make sense of it, through our *being in the world*, then a shift in our mode of being will necessarily give rise to a different world. (2)

The mode of *being in the world* that brings with it the experience of the imaginal is akin to Jung's active imagination and Bachelard's poetic reverie, as a form of idleness or play that is nevertheless intentional. Corbin speaks of imaginative perception, pointing at a form of engagement that is more receptive than creative. Romanyshyn appropriates John Keat's *negative capability*, that ability "of being in uncertainties, mysteries, doubts, without any irritable reaching after fact and reason."

When we are in this mode of being in the world, the separation between subject and object is dissolved in a form of *participation mystique*. Objects become subjects, and the shapeless archetypal figures appear as persons. Personifying is a necessary step in the process of approaching the imaginal. In a world of subjects relationship is possible. We are now able to engage with what would otherwise appear as inanimate outer reality or as inner figments of the imagination, as partners in conversation. We have accessed a mythic consciousness, a liminal zone in which the concepts of inner and outer cease to operate.

The kind of attention that the soul requires is an aesthetic response, a sensing that notices its qualities, more than trying to define or explain away its meaning. As a way of thinking that we associate with the primitive and the insane, it requires a temporary suspension of judgment. Phenomenology's vindication of the subjective experience comes to our rescue. In dealing with the figures of the psyche, we can attend to their phenomenology without being concerned with their ontology. It is none of our business whether or not they are factually real, but the fact that we can experience them as such.

The imaginal approach is a softening in one's perception to make way for a mythic mode of consciousness that accommodates uncertainties. It is a more receptive and less judgmental way of being in the world, in which we give ourselves permission to address and be addressed by the voices of the soul, to engage them as partners in conversation.

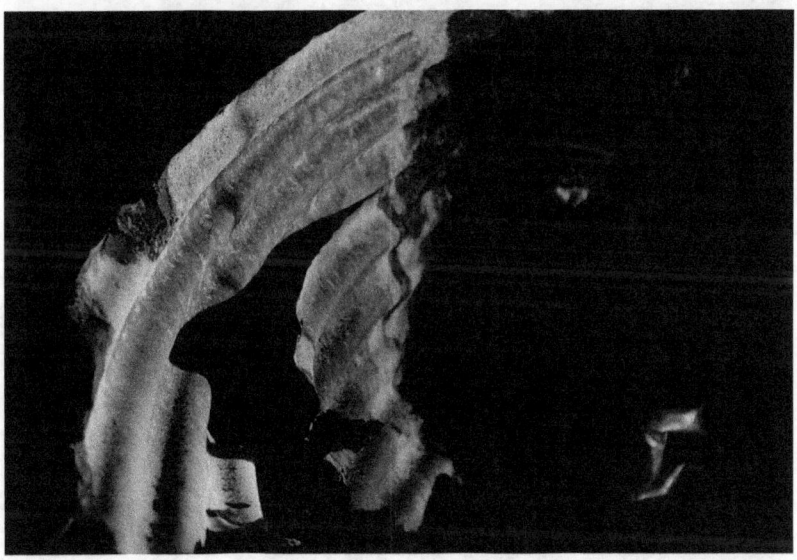

Just as we do not fabricate our dreams but they happen to us, the figures of the psyche have their own autonomy. Cave. Photograph by Carolina Diaz.

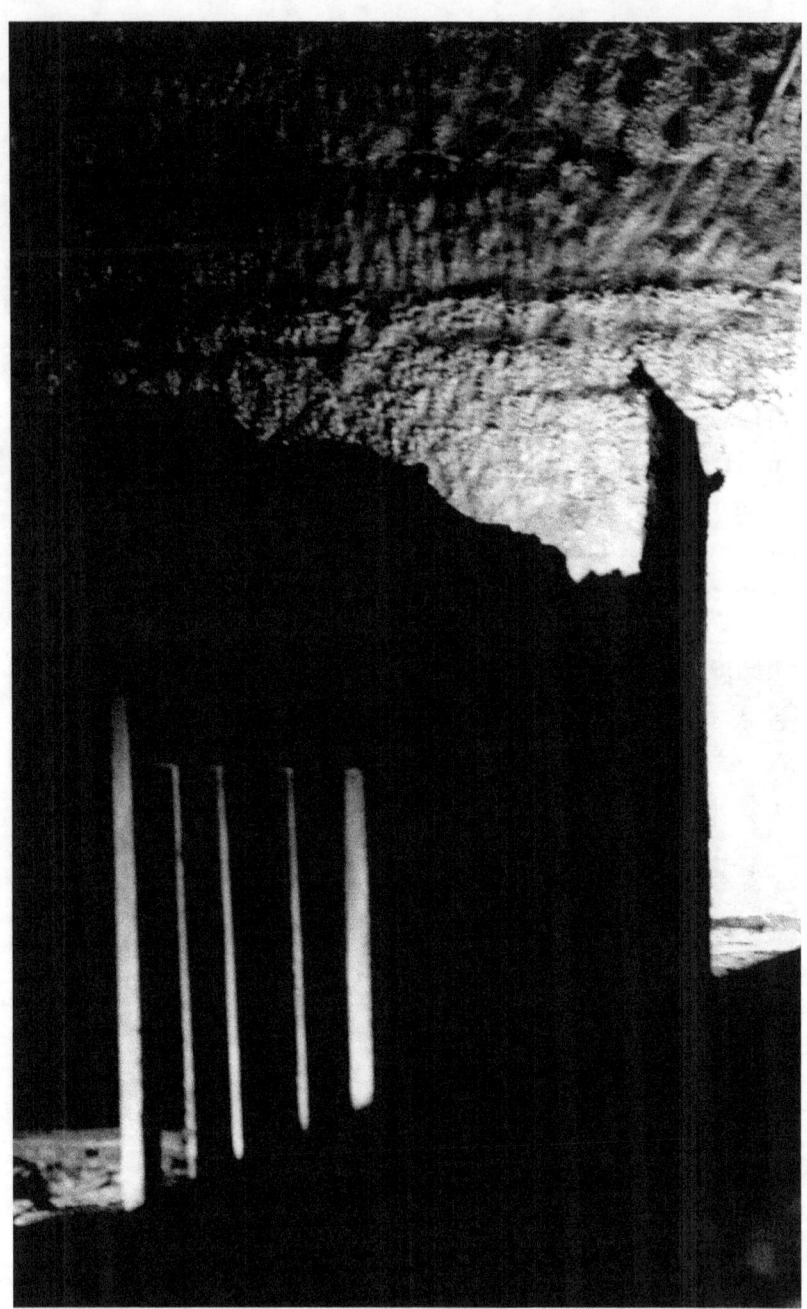

Louise Kenward's *Cave*. Photograph by Carolina Diaz.

2. Bringing light into the darkness: Louise Kenward's *Cave*

For *Cave*, photographer and site-specific artist Louise Kenward spent time occupying a disused space at the back of a shop in East Sussex. The space, with a vaulted ceiling, brick walls and no windows, sits against the cliff face, the rock forming its back wall. Originally used as storage and deposit of discarded objects and debris, it had remained closed and untouched for more than forty years, becoming a sort of time-capsule, before the artist re-opened it in January 2011.

Louise would stay in it for intervals of three hours at a time, once a week, for a period originally set to three months, which got in the end extended to six. During this period, a series of artefacts were retrieved, but the artist insists that the work was the time spent, everything else standing as instruments for documentation and reflection. Louise Kenward's *Cave* is the journey of her relationship with a place.

I am in Hastings' seafront, in a gifts shop that looks more like a set for a Brothers Quay's film. After negotiating my way through its many curiosities, I go through a back door into the place that Louise calls Cave. It is dank and there is no natural light. The atmosphere is oppressive. I want to go further but I am finding it difficult. I stop at the threshold. Louise takes my hand assisting my journey. We walk carefully over pieces of scrap metal, avoiding the stagnant water on the floor. The junk pieces form a messy structure, at one time bridge and palisade, more a deterrent than an invitation. The space they had been shielding from sight is finally revealed. Like a priestess leading an initiate into the sancta sanctorum, Louise takes me into the heart of the Cave: a small clear area where the broken remains of a chair are dimly lit by a portable spotlight. And then something changes. I begin to notice the dripping water has a particular musicality; the moving shadows inspire a sense of reverence; the vaults make the structure resemble a gothic chapel. In a matter of minutes, the dump is transfigured into sacred space. I am still here but it is as if I had suddenly arrived in a different place.

I am reminded of the experience of the *wrong place*, described by Miwon Kwon[3] as somewhere one never inteded to go to and where one feels alienated, in contrast to that of the *right place*, the space of the familiar or comforting. The difference is that in this case both the *wrong* and the *right* places are contained in the same location and at the same time, as if co-existing in parallel levels of reality. What makes this *wrong* place *right* is a certain attitude in the artist that endows it with value, and which is not improvised or forced on, but the product of a long process of endurance that has been more transformative for the artist than for the actual physical place. Her presence consecrates this space. It is pertinent to mention that Louise's interventions were minimal, abiding by a self-imposed rule of not bringing in anything 'apart from light and self'.[4]

It isn't easy to be in this place. Instinctively, I reach for my camera, shelter myself behind it, place it in-between. Through the lens, I can read the daunting space from a safer distance. A protection almost, a charm of sorts.

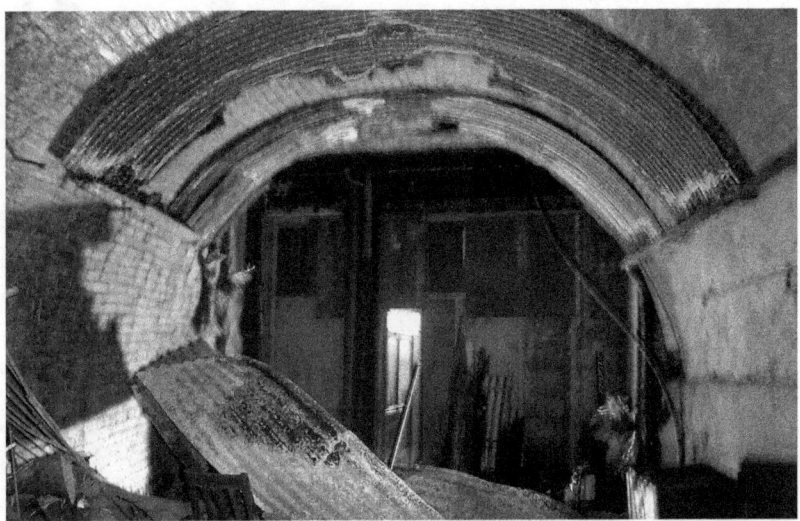

In a matter of minutes, the dump is transfigured into sacred space. I am still here but it is as if I had suddenly arrived in a different place. Cave. Photograph by Louise Kenward

I am thinking of the artist's role as mediator. The term mediated experience has become synonym for the decadent disconnectedness of our times. But all shared experience, all communication is inevitably mediated. Maybe some experiences need to be mediated, facilitated. In the case of the *numinous*, mediation is necessary for two things: connection and distance, both indispensable for creative engagement. Too far removed and a bridge cannot be built. Too close and we are overwhelmed, the bridge gets shattered. So mediation, as in the case of my camera or Louise's guiding hand, creates distance but perhaps a necessary distance that actually facilitates connection. A bridge at one time unites and separates. The same way, the artist as mediator, as intermediary, at one time brings the experience close and separates us from it. The traditional role of the priest, the priestess, the shaman, the witch, to provide the necessary connection and the necessary distance for us to engage with the invisible.

As children of the Enlightenment, we have inherited an ideal of rationality as the light that would dispel all mysteries. But a consciousness that banishes the mystery is not the same as one that understands it; the mystery is simply gone. If we seek to understand the mystery, we have to stay with it. Louise's lamps, literally and metaphorically, did precisely this. What is suggested here is a different kind of light, a different kind of consciousness, that would not dispel the mysteries but rather would embrace them and be with them. The word she kept repeating was 'respect'. She was very careful to introduce just the minimun amount of light that would bring the cave's shadows to life, so they could speak to her.

Louise engaged her *Cave* as a partner in conversation. A practising psychotherapist, she compares the interaction that was established betwen her and *Cave* with the therapeutic relationship. Her main occupation was that of listening, both in a literal and a metaphorical way. She would simply sit there, allowing the mystery of the site to unfold in its own way and at its own pace, showing the patience and the ability to dwell in uncertainty that characterise *negative capability.*

Later that day I am still taken by my experience of Cave. Is this the artist's Cave or could this be anobody's Cave: a neglected, barred, dank place that we all carry within, at the back of the shop —the place where we go about our daytime business? I wonder whether I would have Louise's patience towards my own dark inner places, the patience of just being there and listening.

Giving *Cave* a right to reply, Kenward placed strips of paper on the floor, allowing the dripping water, dirt, flood and living creatures to leave traces. The series of drawings produced as a result, show an attempt to treat the space, not as a thing but almost as a person, a partner in conversation. Personifying is, according to Hillman, essential for engaging the relational, caring aspects of soul as *anima*. When we anima-te the world through an imaginal approach, a personifying, poetic consciousness, we are no longer caught in an instrumental appreciation, the subject-object separation is overcome. We recognise the subjectivity in the world, the world as subject, and the difference is that then we care. For Dewey '... the poetical, in whatever medium, is always a close kin to the animistic.' [5]

At the end of the process, Kenward wrote a goodbye letter, addressed to 'Dear *Cave*', marking the end of a period that was 'at times a sanctuary and at others a curse'. This final gesture provides a retrospective framework to look at the level of personal investment the artist put into this relationship and the caring quality of it.

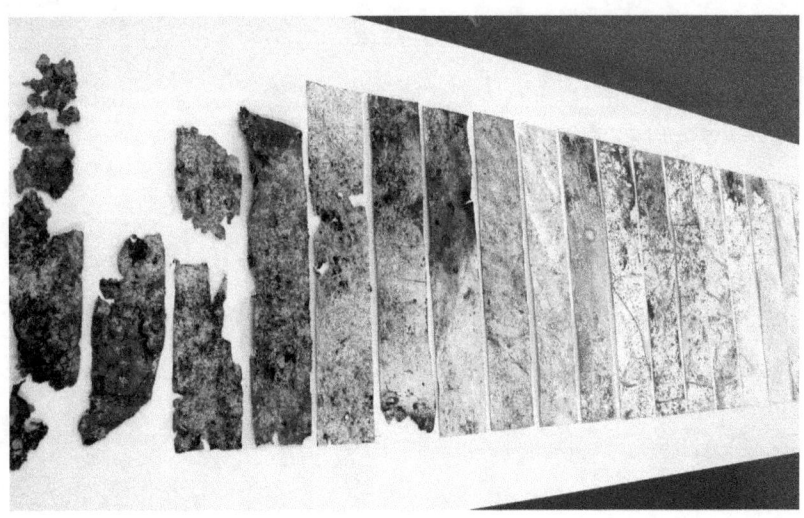

Giving Cave a right to reply. Cave's 'drawings'. Photograph by Louise Kenward

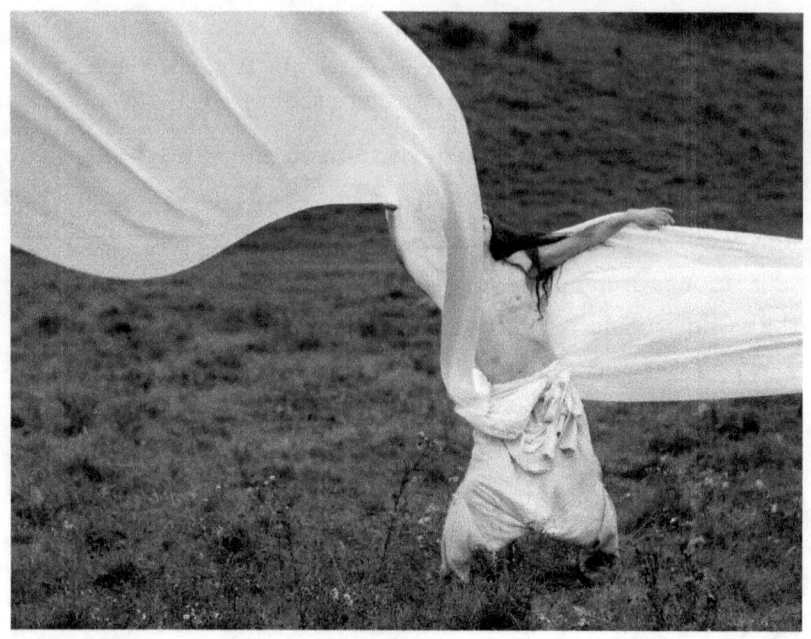

Atsushi Takenouchi in *Chalk.* Photograph by Carolina Diaz

3. Bringing darkness out into the light: Atsushi Takenouchi's *Jinen* Butoh

We are up in the South Downs, just before the sun sets. An audience estimated in some 150 people are being guided down a drover's path and into the valley by performers banging cowbells and uttering calls. After the choir interprets 17th century herding songs, we finally get to see the much anticipated main performer. A deep, gutural scream emerges from the woodland. My skin immediately reacts in goosebumps long before I can even start to think about it. When my rational thinking finally catches up, I realise the thoughts of animal and rites of fertility are already floating in my mind for no reason I can explain. Atsushi Takenouchi appears holding a pair of antlers. This device, althought still subtle, now seems unnecessary, the message of his animal embodiment has already been conveyed by the depth of his voice, reaffirmed by his presence and the energetic quality of his movements.

Originally known as Ankoku Butoh (dance of darkness), Butoh (sometimes Buto or Butō) is a form of postmodern dance theatre initiated in Japan by Tatsumi Hijikata and Kazuo Ohno in 1959, rooted in the tradition of German Expressionism through Mary Wigman and inspired by the political and psychological concerns of Surrealism and existentialist Theatre of the Absurd.[6]

Butoh is a non-representational form of performance. The aim of the dancer is not to represent, to look like, but to *become*, to embody. As an artist in the tradition of Hijikata and Ohno, Takenouchi is more concerned with the embodiment of emotion and image than with the technicalities of dance. Atsushi calls his method *embracing*, and adds the word *Jinen* to his personal approach to Butoh. The Japanese expression *Jinen* brings together the bright and dark aspects of nature and the interconnectedness of all things.

As a student of Takenouchi's since 2005, I have experienced firsthand his methods of *embracing* and *becoming*. Just as 'the aim of the archetypalist is to unveil the images that are already there'[7] Butoh dancers speak of revealing the dance that is already happening, not only in their own bodies but in the universe as a whole. This immanent dance, sometimes defined as *nikutai* or inner landscape[8] can be seen as another way of approaching the imaginal or archetypal dimensions of the soul. Butoh's *becoming* is an embodiment of the phenomenological view that erases the barrier between subject and object, self and other.

Tatsumi Hijikata wanted to become the voice of the socially marginalised: criminals, homosexuals, women and the insane. This idea became expanded by Kazuo Ohno to include the silenced, marginalised voices of the soul: the sister or brother within, the dead, the unborn and the ancestors. Takenouchi embraces all these presences, including those of animals, natural phenomena and places, lending his body for these *others* to have a voice.

Corralled by other performers clashing big cymbals, Atsushi is forced into the passage of an installation built with natural materials. [9] We have been told this performance is inspired by ancient deer hunting practices. I can only describe Atsushi's ucompromising

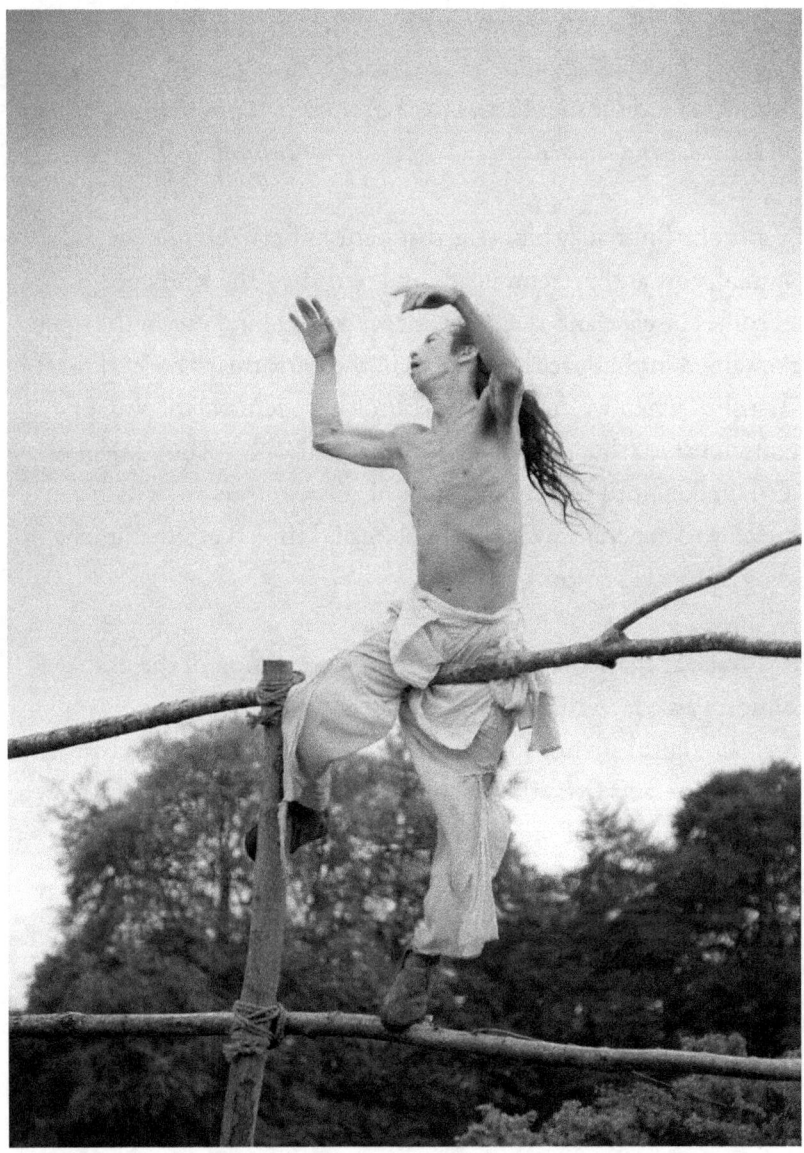

Revealing the dance that is already happening. Atsushi Takenouchi in *Chalk.*
Photograph by Carolina Diaz

*and risqué attitude, negotiating his way across a succession of large
bonfires, as that of someone on the verge of life and death. It brings
images beyond the literalisation of a deer hunt. I am thinking of Jesus
on the cross and the general idea of the sacrifice lamb.*

Butoh's liminality blurs the distinctions between human and
animal, past and present, inside and outside. The landscape
becomes inscape and the interiority is to be found out in the open,
contained in the space as much as in the performer's body. For
Atsushi, "when we dance *Jinen* [Butoh], we remove the wall of
consciousness that perceives the individual 'I'"[10] The audience
also is taken into that liminal state of consciousness in which we
are able to experience this other place and time that inhabits the
geographical location.

It is clear that Chalk is not the literal recreation of the past.
Simon Pascoe, co-director of the piece and Dr. Matt Pope,
archaeological advisor for the project, reveal that access to historical
data or artefacts from the site was very limited; not much is known
about the history of the place. In addition to that, the dancer is
Japanese and his style contemporary, there are singers interpreting
Russian and Mongolian folk songs.[11] These elements clearly do
not belong to the history of this landscape, but their presences
combine seamlessly with it, the effect is anything but artifice. What
Chalk is restoring is not the factual past but an imaginal ancestry,
which then takes on a more universal, timeless resonance.

Timelessness is central to Butoh's ethos, in which characters exist
in a permanent state of transition, ever-changing, fluid, forever
transmuting into something else. 'Butoh exists in mythological
time. It could be any time, because characterization never solidifies.'[12]

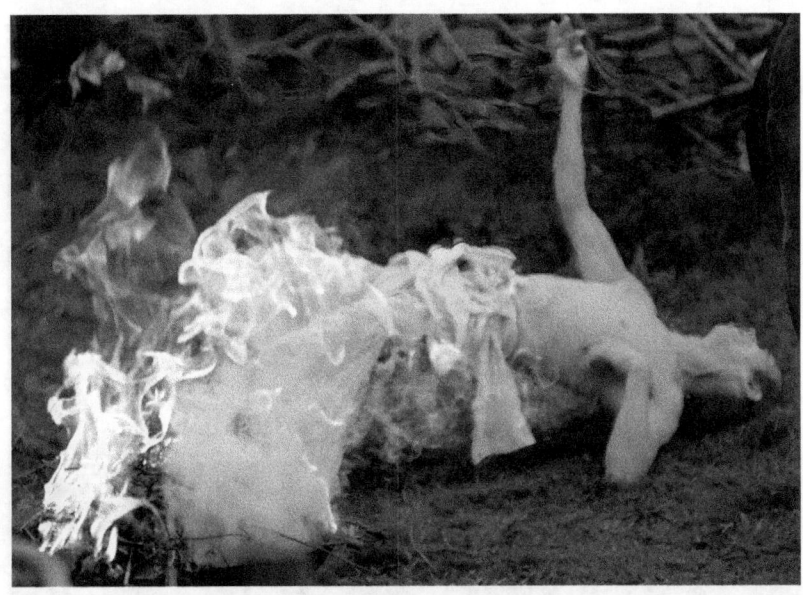

Atsushi's uncompromising attitude, as someone on the verge of life and death. Chalk.
Photograph by Carolina Diaz

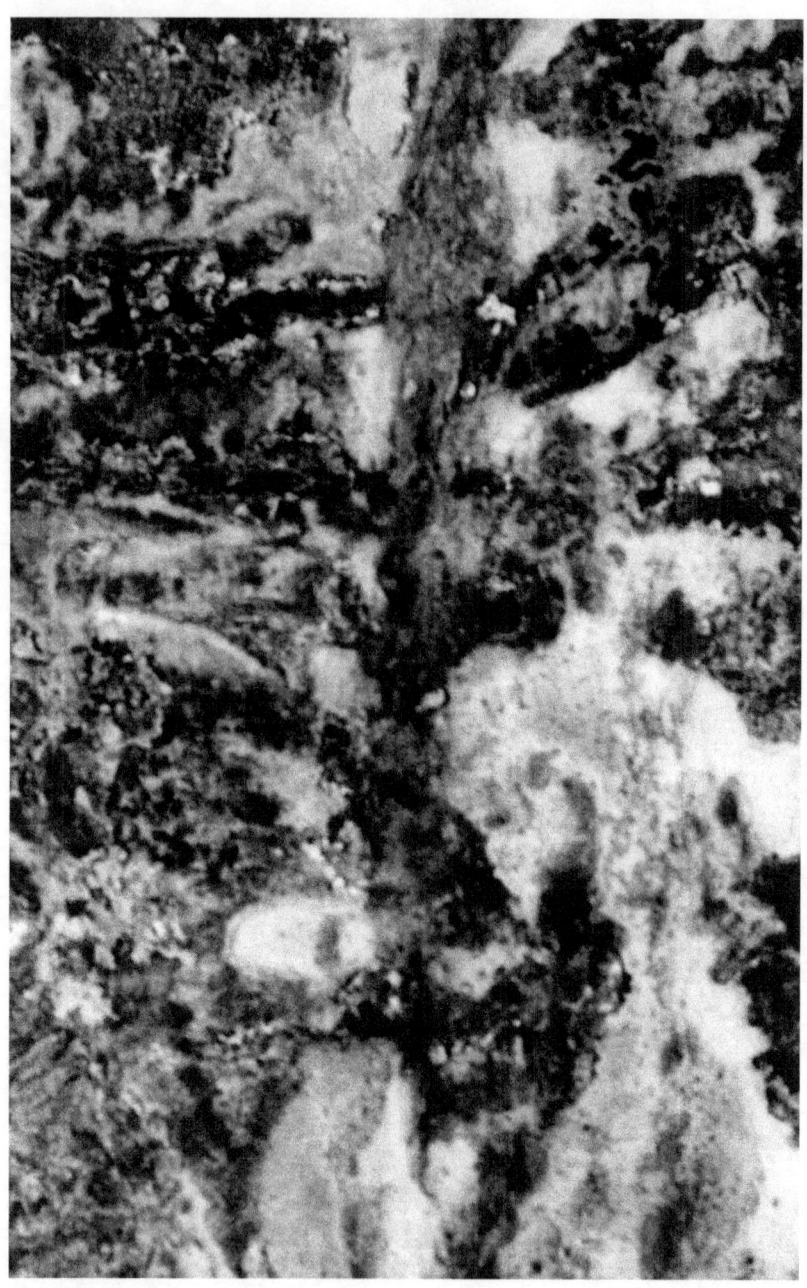

Louise Kenward's *Cave.* Photograph by Carolina Diaz

4. An imaginal approach to arts practice as cultural-historical therapeutics

The mythic-archetypal consciousness that forms the basis for an imaginal approach to arts practice does not ask for the literal restoration of images from the past, but of the mythical, symbolic quality in the present experiencing of life. Its concern is not with formal choices or particular subject matters but with an attitude that informs a process-led creation in which the artist becomes more the agent through whom the work comes into being than its source. By allowing the work to fulfill its own purpose, something beyond the artist's personal ego can speak through it.

This approach is about remaining receptive, more passive than active, more to do with listening and waiting. A process more akin to gestation than creation. This is not about controlling the materials, this is not about subordinating the work to the artist's conscious intentions. Instead, it is about surrendering these intentions and actions to the soul of the work, to its own aims, which will eventually be revealed, rather than imposed by a conscious plan.

I find examples of this particular attitude in Louise Kenward's relational practice and in Atsushi Takenouchi's *Jinen* Butoh. Different as they are, the approaches of these two artists seem to share a common concern for something other than their personal intentions, an openness to being addressed and being at the service of something *other*.

Kenward enters into personal relationships with the places she inhabits; Takenouchi embraces the dead, the ancestors and the natural phenomena, embodying them. Both devote their practices to giving these presences a voice. These gestures resonate in the viewer's mind in subtle but powerful ways. We can say with Butoh founder Kazuo Onho that 'our dance becomes godlike once the ghosts of the universe surge forth from the depths of our consciousness.'[13] His assertion is of course extensive to any medium.

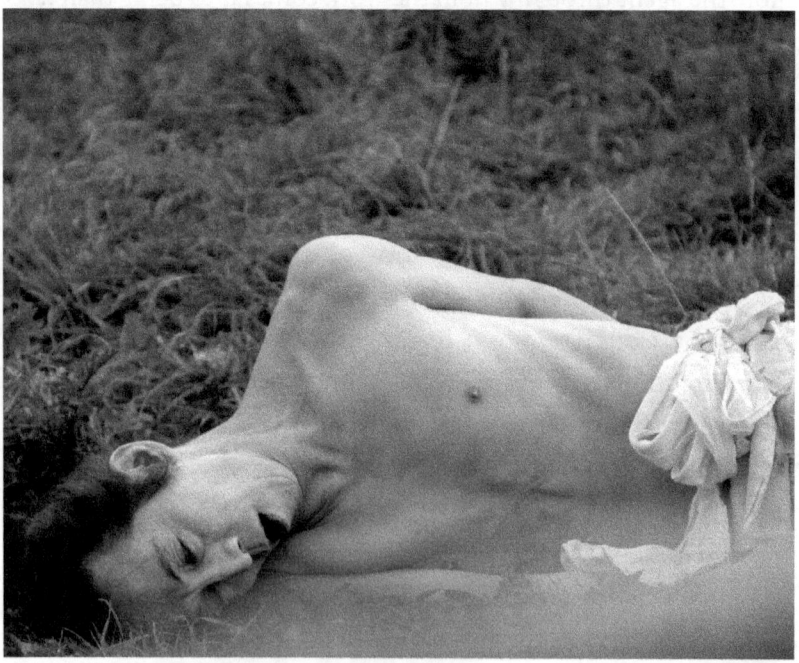

Atsushi Takenouchi. *Chalk.* Photograph by Carolina Diaz

The archetypal nature of the soul is both instinctual and divine. By accessing this deeper dimension, these works become intermediaries for the sacred, not as dogma or cultural construct, but as an aspect of reality that can be experienced directly.

Soul is also about connections, it is about our relationships, in the realms of the personal, the inter-personal and the trans-personal, both visible and invisible, within and without. Engaging with the invisible world of the psychic presences is not at odds with an active engagement with the world. On the contrary, the cultivation of the relational aspects of the soul dissolves the instrumental perception of nature and *other* as objects, establishing what in phenomenological discourse is known as an *intersubjective* world.[14] This approach can form the basis for a practice that is more socially and ecologically aware.

Both Kenward's *Cave* and Takenouchi's *Jinen* Butoh explore a liminal zone that challenges our conceptions of inside and outside. They are, as Romanyshyn would put it, 'inner journeys in the outer world'.[15] More than anything else, their work is transformative at various levels.

In search of a broader definition of sustainable art or art for sustainability, we need to take one step beyond the practical direct effects on social, political and environmental issues.

If what remains unconscious manifests as symptoms, as Jung once pointed out, what remains collectively supressed becomes collective cultural disease. The role played by the unconscious should be part of the discussion on sustainability. An art in service of a sustainable future, an art that *sustains* us, that helps us re-establish balance, would need to extend our relational field into the unconscious and the wild: nature out there and nature within.

By participating in the global task of 'making the unconscious of humanity more conscious' they become part of what Romanyshyn would call an 'ongoing cultural-historical therapeutics'.[16]

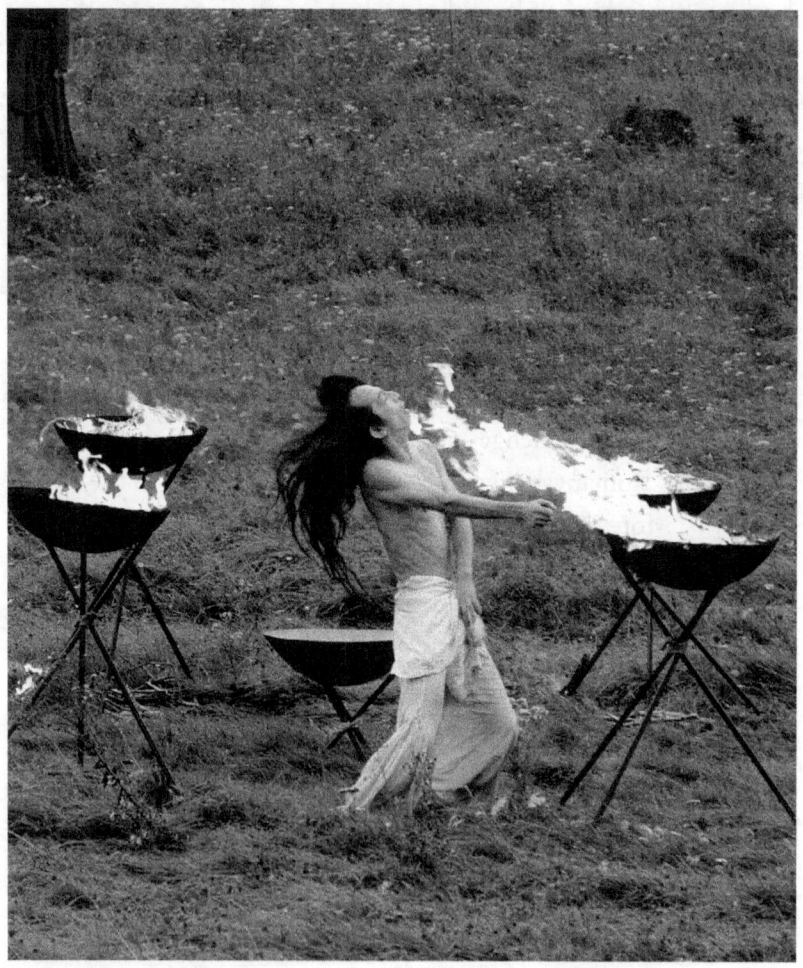

Atsushi Takenouchi. *Chalk.* Photograph by Carolina Diaz

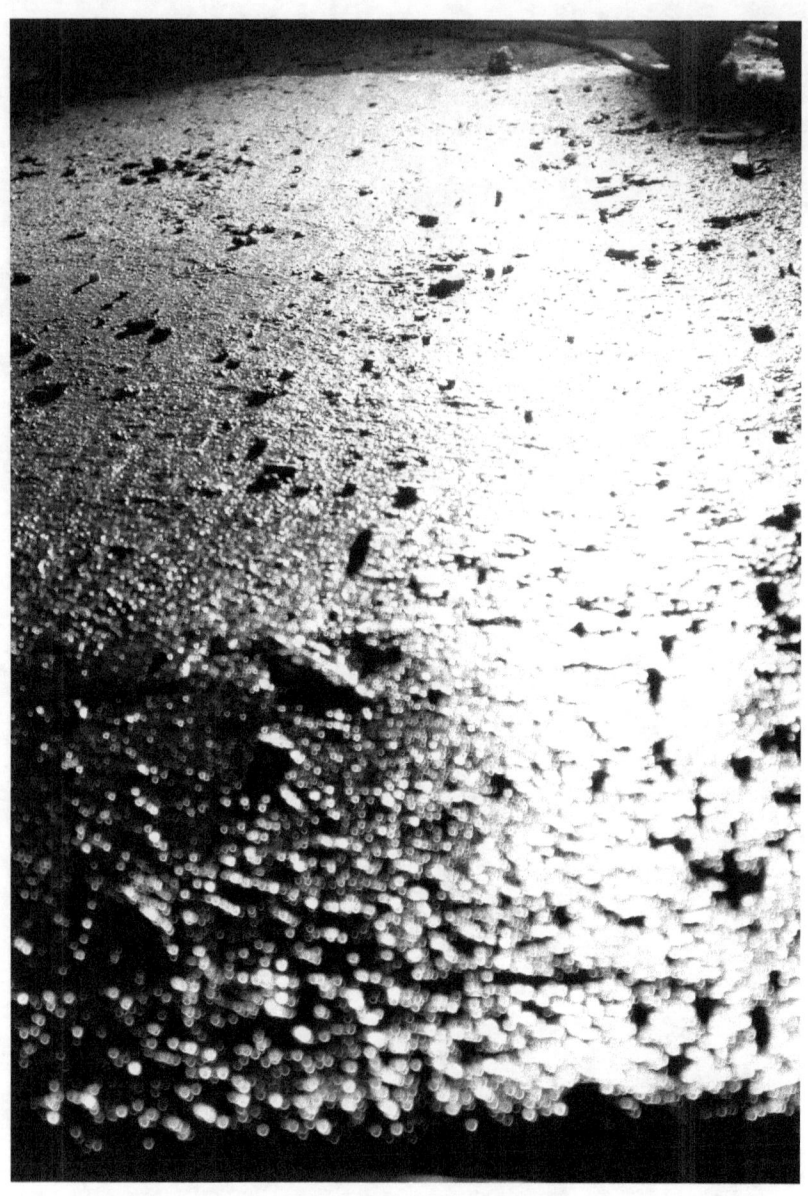

An art for a sustainable future would need to extend our relational field into the unconscious and the wild: nature out there and nature within. Cave. Photograph by Carolina Diaz

Conclusion

By looking at the works of the two artists discussed, through the lens of the imaginal, I hope to have shown that there are ways of making a place for the unconscious, the mythical and the soul in arts practice that are relevant to the concerns of our contemporary world. These two pieces prove the point that the restoration of a mythic consciousness within the arts does not need to be confined to certain motives or formal tendencies; that spiritual preoccupations are not circumscribed within particular styles or moments in history but, on the contrary, being part of our constitution are pertinent at any time.

The practices of these two artists become a form of *soul-making* by providing a vehicle for the archetypal, for the invisible to manifest in the world. What this type of work heals is not immediate, but subtle and cumulative: the ongoing relationship between the cultural consciousness and the figures of the collective unconscious. Whether or not the artists acknowledge this, or call it that name, is irrelevant. We do not need to sympathise with the ideas of C.G. Jung, James Hillman or Robert Romanyshyn to recognise the reality and importance of a whole area of our experience to which we are entitled as living beings. I am sure the artists will not be offended when I affirm that their work is devoted to the soul.

They are both examples of the kind of devotional attitude that Suzi Gablik perceived as missing in the postmodern arts.[17] The devotional attitude challenges an instrumental view of the world and of everything that is perceived as *other* : body, female, nature, other persons, other cultures, other species. The devotional attitude humbles the artist by shifting her role from subject that observes and makes use of resources outside of herself, to an embodied being that establishes relationships and experiences the other as partner in conversation.

This type of work is not about religion but about recuperating our religious sensibility as poetic consciousness. It is about reclaiming the right to ask big questions, to bring in the fundamental issues of life back into the arts debate, about re-acquiring a taste for depth.

Just as I write this, and perhaps by no coincidence, I come across an article in Jonathan Jones's art blog in The Guardian,[18] where he rants on about the role the artists have played in the last decades in the rise of the decadent values of consumerism, through their exaltation of the shallow and the banal: 'everywhere, emotional depth in art was censored'... 'The modern world has screwed itself and art led the way.' If our creative work can have such an impact on society, superficiality can indeed be a dangerous business.

'Art for art's sake or art for society's sake?' [18] Gablik's question suggests these two alternatives exist in mutually exclusive opposition. The only choice seems to be either pleasing oneself or pleasing the audience. A shift from the perspective of the ego to that of the soul is a way of finding a middle path, a third that resolves what otherwise looks like two opposites that could never meet. *Art for soul's sake* is at once individual and collective. It is a form of service that is nevertheless experienced as deeply personal; without being narcissistic, it is uncompromising.

Arts practice with soul in mind is a way of acknowledging the responsibility that we acquire by placing the products of our creativity in the public arena. Once out there, they are not only our own, they become the ingredients with which culture builds itself. By choosing to go public, the artist becomes 'collective man – one who carries and shapes the unconscious, psychic life of mankind.'[19]

Perhaps the role of the artist that undertakes this task is more akin to that of the *shaman*, that visits other realms in order to heal our relationship to them. Explorers of the imaginal world, they perform these excursions not for themselves but for others. In choosing to become mediators in the public sphere, their acts go beyond the personally therapeutic, beyond the healing of individual history and into the framework of collective, cultural history. In a subtle but deep way, these acts become a practice in cultural-historical therapeutics. By addressing the intimacy of the soul and dissolving the barriers between inside and outside, they become ways of participating in the global task of *soul-making*, in the healing of the very fabric of the universe.

Notes

1. See Suzi Gablik 1984, 1992, 1995.

2. Maurice Merleau-Ponty 1945

3. Miwon Kwon 2002

4. Louise Kenward, interviewed by the author on 20th November 2011 at Towner Gallery, Eastbourne.

5. John Dewey 1934

6. For more on the history of Butoh and its performers, see Fraleigh 1999, 2004, Fraleigh and Nakamura 2006, Iwana 2011, Ohno and Ohno 2004 and Roquet 2004.

7. James Hillman 1989

8. Masaki Iwana 2011

9. It refers to the temporary installation *River* by Red Earth. Harting Down, Sussex, 2011.

10. Atsushi Takenouchi in Fraleigh and Nakamura 2006

11. Simon Pascoe and Matt Pope interviewed in *Making History*. See BBC4 2011.

12. Sondra Fraleigh 1999

13. Kazuo Ohno in Ohno and Ohno 2004

14. Maurice Merleau-Ponty 1945

15. Robert Romanyshyn 2011

16. Robert Romanyshyn 2007

17. Suzi Gablik 1984

18. Jonathan Jones . "How art killed our culture: all the shallowness of modern mass culture began in avant-garde art 40 years ago." *The Guardian.* 6 March 2009
http://www.guardian.co.uk/artanddesign/jonathanjonesblog/2009/mar/06

19. C.G. Jung 1933

Bibliography

- Bachelard, G. (1964) *The poetics of space*. Maria Jolas (trans.) Boston: Beacon.
- Bachelard, G. (1969) *The poetics of reverie: childhood, language and the cosmos*. Daniel Russell (trans.) Boston: Beacon.
- Dewey, J. (1934) *Art as experience*. New York : Paragon.
- Fraleigh, S. (1999) *Dancing into darkness : Butoh, Zen and Japan*. Pittsburgh : University of Pittsburgh Press.
- Fraleigh, S. (2004) *Dancing identity : metaphysics in motion*. Pittsburgh: University of Pittsburgh Press.
- Fraleigh, S. and Nakamura, T. (2006) *Hijikata Tatsumi and Ohno Kazuo*. New York: Routledge.
- Gablik, S. (1984) *Has modernism failed?* London: Thames and Hudson.
- Gablik, S. (1992) *The reenchantment of art*. London: Thames and Hudson.
- Gablik, S. (1995) *Conversations before the end of time: dialogues on art, life and spiritual renewal*. London: Thames and Hudson.
- Hauke, C. (2000) *Jung and the postmodern: the interpretation of realities*. London: Routledge.
- Hillman, J. (1975) *Re-visioning psychology*. New York : Harper Collins.
- Hillman, J. and Moore, T. (1989) *A blue fire: selected writings by James Hillman*. New York: Harper Collins.
- Iwana, M. (2011) *The intensity of nothingness: the dance and thoughts of Masaki Iwana*. 2nd. ed. Réveillon: La Maison du Butoh Blanc.
- Jung, C. G. (1933) *Modern man in search of a soul*. London: Harvest
- Jung, C.G. (1963) *Memories, dreams, reflections*. Aniela Jaffé (ed.) Richard and Clara Winston (trans.) London: Routledge.
- Kwon, M. (2002) *One place after another*. Boston : MIT Press.
- Matthews, E. (2002) *The philosophy of Merleau-Ponty*. Chesham : Acumen.
- Merleau-Ponty, M. (1945) *Phenomenology of perception*. New York : Routledge.
- Ohno, K and Ohno, Y. (2004) *Kazuo Ohno's world from without and within*. Trans. John Barrett. Middletown : Wesleyan University.

- Romanyshyn, R. (2001) *Mirror and metaphor: images and stories of psychological life*. Pittsburgh: Trivium. [Originally published in 1982 as Psychological life: from science to metaphor, Texas: University of Texas]
- Romanyshyn, R. (2002) *Ways of the heart: essays toward an imaginal psychology*. Pittsburgh: Trivium.
- Romanyshyn, R. (2007) *The wounded researcher : research with soul in mind*. New Orleans : Spring Journal.
- Roquet, P. (2004) Towards the bowels of the earth : Butoh writhing [sic] in perspectives. 2nd. rev. ed. Davis, CA. : Palupalu.20

ARTICLES
- Cashford, J. (2011) *The myth of the messenger.* Aras Connections. Issue 3. ARAS, The Archive for Research in Archetypal Symbolism. http://aras.org [last accessed: 26 November 2011]
- Corbin, H. (1972) *Mundus imaginalis or the imaginary and the imaginal.* Ruth Horine (trans.) Zürich. [Extract from paper originally delivered at the Colloquium on symbolism in Paris, June 1964. First published in Cahiers Internationaux de Symbolisme 6, Brussels, 1964, pp. 3-26] in: http://www.scribd.com/doc/21749897/MUNDUS-IMAGINALIS [accessed: 25 September 2011]
- Gablik, S. (1998) *The nature of beauty in contemporary art.* New Renaissance.Vol.8,No 1
- Gordon, H. & Tamari, S. (2004) *Maurice Merleau-Ponty's phenomenology of perception : a basis for sharing the earth.* Contributions in Philosophy, No. 89. Westport : Praeger.
- Hung, R. *Educating for and through nature: a Merleau-Pontian approach.* e-article. Springer Science+Business Media B.V. 2007
- Jones, J. (2009) *How art killed our culture: all the shallowness of modern mass culture began in avant-garde art 40 years ago.* Jonathan Jones on Art Blog.The Guardian. 6 March. http://www. guardian.co.uk/artanddesign/jonathanjonesblog/2009/mar/06 [accessed: 29 November 2011]
- Unstructured 4. *Land, sea and sky: Red Earth's Seven Sisters ritual performance.* http://www. fourthdoor.co.uk. [accessed: 23 November 2011]
- Wright, J. (2006) *Honoring both worlds: visible and invisible.* Jung Society Newsletter. Spring. Atlanta: C.G.Jung Society. http://www.jungatlanta.com [accesed: 7 November 2011]

MEDIA
- NHK Enterprises (2006) *Kazuo Ohno long interview.* Yokohama [Video: DVD] (Interview with Kazuo Ohno by Toru Fukui, 1993. Trans. John A. Barrett)
- BBC4 (2011) *Making History.* 4 Oct, 15:00. (Review of Chalk by Martin Ellis, with

interviews to Simon Pascoe and Matt Pope). [Radio: online].
- Romanyshyn, R. (2011) *Inner journeys in the outer world: melting polar ice.* Lecture. 08 September
2011. Jung Platform [Video: online].
http://viewer.dacast.com/broadcaster/jungplatform/romanyshyn-talk-h264
[accessed: 2 November 2011]
- Samuels, A. (1995) *Jung and the post-jungians.* Leicester University. [video interview: online]
http://www.andrewsamuels.com [accessed: 1 November 2011]

INTERVIEW
- Diaz, C. (2011) Louise Kenward. Towner Gallery, Eastbourne, 20 November 2011.
[interview]

VISITS
- Louise Kenward. *Cave.* Hastings, 24 September 2011.
- Red Earth. *River* installation and *Chalk* performance (Atsushi Takenouchi). Harting Down,
25 September 2011.

OTHER PRINTED SOURCES
- Kenward, L. (2011) *Self, space and objects: relational practice through the experience of spaces.* Critical
evaluative report. The Cass School of Art, London Metropolitan University.
- Red Earth (2011) *Chalk: installation, performance, ritual.* [Performance programme]
- Creative Coast (2011) *Coastal Currents: visual arts festival 2011.* Hastings. [Catalogue]

ONLINE RESOURCES
- Jinen Butoh. Atsushi Takenouchi's website. http://www.jinen-butoh.com
- Louise Kenward's website: http://www.louisekenward.com
- Red Earth's website. http://www.redearth.co.uk
- Robert Romanyshyn's website. http://robertromanyshyn.com
- The Jung Page: Reflections on Psychology, Culture and Life. http://www.cgjungpage.org

Atsushi Takenouchi is a Japanese butoh performer. His formative period included direct influence from butoh founders Tatsumi Hijikata and Kazuo Ohno. He has been dancing his own Jinen Butoh since 1986, performing and teaching all around the world. Partner and collaborator Hiroko Komiya provides the soundscapes to dances that explore the natural and urban worlds, the light and darkness in inner and outer nature. His workshops welcome participants with any level of skill, from beginners to professionals, as well as children and participants with disabilities.

Chalk by the multimedia group Red Earth comprised a series of installations and performances in open landscape in the South Downs, realised between April and October 2011. Atsushi Takenouchi's performances took place in two locations: Harting Down and Wolstonbury Hill, on September 24th-25th and October 8th-9th.

Louise Kenward is a photographer, performance artist and psychotherapist. Her work explores "the betwixt and between of the liminal... with regards to the physical spaces we inhabit and the mental spaces we dwell." She holds an MA in Fine Art from The Cass School of Art and a Foundation degree from Brighton University. Louise currently lives and works between Bexhill and Hastings, East Sussex.

Cave happened at the back of Pier Shop in Arthur Greens, White Rock, Hastings TN34 1JU East Sussex. The artist's inhabiting period started in January 2011. It was opened to the public from 27th August until 30th September 2011, as part of the *Spotlight: Open* programme of the local Coastal Currents festival.

About the author:

Carolina Diaz is a visual artist and dancer. Her current practice integrates artist's books, photography, live performance and dance for the camera. Her book *Dance for the page* has been included in the Tate Library's special collection. She has studied and practised Butoh since 2005, creating solo work and collaborating with dancers, sound artists and film makers, in improvisation and choreographed pieces. She is based in Sussex.

www.ingramcontent.com/pod-product-compliance
Lightning Source LLC
Chambersburg PA
CBHW071646170526
45166CB00003B/1459